M000226462

To

_____

From

_____

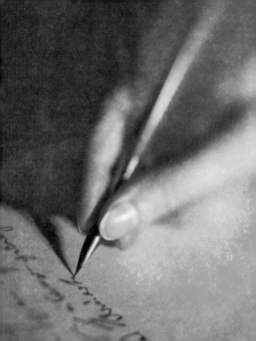

Jane Austen

Speaks to Women

Edith Lank

Andrews McMeel
Publishing

Kansas City

Jane Austen Speaks to Women

❧

ISBN: 0-7407-1047-8
Library of Congress Catalog Card Number:
00-100443

Contents

Introduction   vii

Girls and Women   1

Men   11

Enjoying Life   17

Dancing and Courtship   21

Marriage   31

Money   39

Right and Wrong   45

Contents

Health   53

Food   57

Letters to Cassandra   61

On Her Writing   75

Growing Old   81

INTRODUCTION

Reading Jane Austen's witty words of wisdom, some written as many as two hundred years ago, women need to remember two things:

She was skilled in letting her characters reveal themselves through their words, so it's helpful to know when something in a novel is being said by a fool or a rascal.

And in addition, much of the time she said things she didn't mean at all. She was a master of irony. Even in letters to her sister Cassandra, she used humor to disguise serious sentiments. Some of her phrases and sentences, standing alone, should be taken with a grain of salt.

Introduction

For example, Jane Austen had her tongue firmly in cheek when she wrote one of the most famous first lines in any English novel:

It is a truth universally acknowledged, that a single man in possession of a good fortune, must be in want of a wife.

                       ❧ narrator *Pride and Prejudice*

And part of the irony is that although she said it with a tolerant chuckle—that's the way the story worked out.

Jane Austen

Speaks to Women

GIRLS AND WOMEN

Young women, learning about the world and about themselves, were Jane Austen's main concern. Two hundred years later, girls haven't changed much, but the world has.

It must be very improper that a young lady should dream of a gentleman before the gentleman is first known to have dreamt of her.

> ❧ narrator, fondly chuckling about our young
> heroine *Northanger Abbey*

1

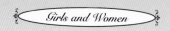

Girls and Women

What young lady . . . will reach the age of sixteen without changing her name as far as she can?

        🍃 narrator, *Northanger Abbey*

[Miss Bates] was a great talker upon little matters.

           🍃 narrator *Emma*

A woman of seven and twenty . . . can never hope to inspire affection again.

      🍃 Marianne Dashwood, at the age of seventeen
           Sense and Sensibility

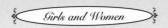

[Miss Bates] enjoyed a most uncommon degree of popularity for a woman neither young, handsome, rich nor married.

> written by the author, who was none of those
> things herself *Emma*

A woman especially, if she have the misfortune of knowing any thing, should conceal it as well as she can.

> narrator, who may have learned that the hard way
> herself *Northanger Abbey*

Young ladies are like delicate plants. They should take care of their health and their complexion.

> ❧ fussy Mr. Woodhouse, who went in deadly fear
> of drafts himself *Emma*

I should no more lay it down as a general rule that women write better letters than men, than that they sing better duets, or draw better landscapes. In every power, of which taste is the foundation, excellence is pretty fairly divided between the sexes.

> ❧ Henry Tilney, demonstrating as we first meet him
> that he will be worthy of young Catherine
> *Northanger Abbey*

[History is] the quarrels of popes and kings, with wars and pestilences, in every page; the men all so good for nothing, and hardly any women at all.

> ❧ young and innocent Catherine Morland, speaking truer than she knew *Northanger Abbey*

As far as I have had opportunity of judging, it appears to me that the usual style of letter-writing among women is faultless, except in three particulars. . . . A general deficiency of subject, a total inattention to stops, and a very frequent ignorance of grammar.

> ❧ Henry Tilney, teasing Catherine ("stops" were punctuation) *Northanger Abbey*

She was not a woman of many words, for unlike people in general, she proportioned them to the number of her ideas.

> ❧ narrator, faintly praising the disagreeable Mrs.
> Ferrars *Sense and Sensibility*

Mrs. Elton, as elegant as lace and pearls could make her.

> ❧ narrator *Emma*

A whole day's tête-à-tête between two women can never end without a quarrel.

> ❧ Caroline Bingley, revealing her feelings about her
> sister *Pride and Prejudice*

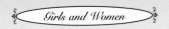

I have been meditating on the very great pleasure which a pair of fine eyes in the face of a pretty woman can bestow.

❧ Mr. Darcy, snubbing a flirt by talking of her rival
Pride and Prejudice

We [women] live at home, quiet, confined, and our feelings prey upon us.

❧ Anne Elliot, explaining why women don't forget lost lovers *Persuasion*

No man can be a good judge of the comfort a woman finds in the society of one of her own sex.

❧ Mrs. Weston *Emma*

[She looks] ill, very ill—that is, if a young lady can ever be allowed to look ill.

         ⋙ Frank Churchill *Emma*

A lady, without [children], was the very best preserver of furniture in the world.

         ⋙ advice to a prospective landlord *Persuasion*

No one can think more highly of the understanding of women than I do . . . nature has given them so much, that they never find it necessary to use more than half.

         ⋙ Henry Tilney, teasing again (we hope)

         Northanger Abbey

It is only by seeing women in their own homes . . . just as they always are, that you can form any just judgment.

> ❧ Frank Churchill, bitter after a quarrel with his
> secret fiancée *Emma*

Daughters are never of so much consequence to a father.

> ❧ the overbearing Lady Catherine
> *Pride and Prejudice*

He knew her illnesses; they never occurred but for her own convenience.

> ❧ Frank Churchill, about his domineering aunt,
> who proceeded to surprise him by dying *Emma*

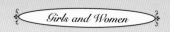

We certainly do not forget you, so soon as you forget us.

        ❧ Anne Elliot, still grieving for a lost love

        after eight years *Persuasion*

A strong sense of duty is no bad part of a woman's portion.

        ❧ Anne Elliot ("portion" meaning dowry)

        Persuasion

. . . the gentlemen perhaps thought each to himself, "Women will have their little nonsenses and needless cares."

        ❧ narrator *Emma*

MEN

Some critics these days see Jane Austen as an early feminist, shyly attacking the patriarchal world she lived in. Others hold that she saw the situation clearly but never thought of rebelling, that she took for granted that some of her brothers would go to Oxford, two rise to the rank of admirals, and another become very rich—while she and her sister Cassandra remained with their parents, managing cheerfully on very little money.

[He had] a face of strong, natural, sterling insignificance.

🖎 narrator *Sense and Sensibility*

Men

He seems a very harmless sort of young man, nothing to like or dislike in him — goes out shooting or hunting . . . all the morning, and plays at whist and makes queer faces in the evening.

letter to Cassandra

Men have had every advantage of us in telling their own story. Education has been theirs in so much higher a degree; the pen has been in their hands.

Anne Elliot Persuasion

He was careless and immethodical, like other men.

Mrs. Smith, in trouble about her late husband's finances Persuasion

Men

He was not an ill-disposed young man, unless to be rather cold hearted, and rather selfish, is to be ill-disposed.

         🐦 narrator, about the heroines' half-brother

                            Sense and Sensibility

Adm. Stanhope is a gentleman-like man, but then his legs are too short and his tail too long.

         🐦 letter to Cassandra

. . . all the minute particulars, which only women's language can make interesting. — In [men's] communications we deal only in the great.

         🐦 Mr. George Knightly, who didn't mean it

                               Emma

Men

[Men] are the most conceited creatures in the world, and think themselves of so much importance!

      flirtatious Isabella Thorpe, who ran after men at every opportunity Northanger Abbey

A man must have a very good opinion of himself when he asks people to leave their own fireside . . . for the sake of coming to see him.

      home-loving John Knightly Emma

The ladies here probably exchanged looks which meant, "Men never know when things are dirty or not."

      narrator Emma

Men

Her father was . . . a very respectable man, though his name was Richard—and he had never been handsome.

> ◆ narrator (the "Richard" must have been an inside family joke; Jane Austen's early works were written for reading aloud evenings to amuse her family)
>
> *Northanger Abbey*

Man is more robust than woman, but he is not longer-lived; which exactly explains my view of the nature of their attachments.

> ◆ Anne Elliot, explaining why women love longest
>
> *Persuasion*

All I want in a man is someone who rides bravely, dances beautifully, sings with vigor, reads passionately, and whose taste agrees in every point with my own.

❧ Marianne Dashwood, full of illusions
at seventeen *Sense and Sensibility*

ENJOYING LIFE

Jane Austen's novels, and particularly her letters, make it clear that, as she says herself, it was not worthwhile waiting for excuses to enjoy oneself.

I had a very pleasant evening . . . though you will probably find out that there was no particular reason for it; but I do not think it worth while to wait for enjoyment until there is some real opportunity for it.

        ❧ letter to her sister Cassandra when Jane was
        twenty-three

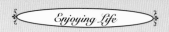

It was a delightful visit;—perfect, in being much too short.

      ❧ narrator *Emma*

My idea of good company . . . is the company of clever, well-informed people, who have a great deal of conversation.

      ❧ Anne Elliot *Persuasion*

A mind lively and at ease can do with seeing nothing, and can see nothing that does not answer.

      ❧ narrator, describing Emma's contented view of a

      quiet village street *Emma*

Perfect happiness, even in memory, is not common.

> ❧ narrator *Emma*

One half of the world cannot understand the pleasures of the other.

> ❧ Emma Woodhouse *Emma*

I am sorry my mother has been suffering, and am afraid this exquisite weather is too good to agree with her. I enjoy it all over me, from top to toe, from right to left, longitudinally, perpendicularly, diagonally.

> ❧ letter to Cassandra (their mother, who outlived Jane by many years, was annoyingly hypochondriac)

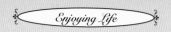

Enjoying Life

To sit in the shade on a fine day and look upon verdure, is the most perfect refreshment.

       ❧ Fanny Price *Mansfield Park*

The person, be it gentleman or lady, who has not pleasure in a good novel, must be intolerably stupid.

       ❧ Henry Tilney *Northanger Abbey*

DANCING AND COURTSHIP

Critics who miss the subtlety of her style sometimes complain that Jane Austen was interested only in trivial matters like courtship and marriage. Today we read novels about careers, travel, and adventure, but in her day, marriage was the only career, the only adventure open to a young woman of her class. Dancing represented a chance for girls to exhibit their charms, perhaps even touch young men's hands. Balls were a vital marriage market.

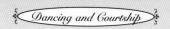

[Frank Churchill] argued like a man very bent on dancing.

          ✒ narrator *Emma*

Mary petitioned for the use of the library at Netherfield; and Kitty begged very hard for a few balls there every winter.

        ✒ narrator *Pride and Prejudice*

It may be possible to do without dancing entirely. Instances have been known of young people passing many months . . . without being at any ball . . . and no material injury accrue . . .

          ✒ narrator *Emma*

To be mistress of French, Italian, German, Music, Singing, Drawing etc., will gain a woman some applause, but will not add one lover to her list.

❧ scheming Susan Vernon *Lady Susan*

There was one gentleman, an officer of the Cheshire, a very good-looking young man, who, I was told, wanted very much to be introduced to me, but as he did not want it quite enough to take much trouble in effecting it, we never could bring it about.

❧ letter to Cassandra

Dancing and Courtship

I am almost afraid to tell you how my Irish friend and I behaved. Imagine to yourself everything most profligate and shocking in the way of dancing and sitting down together.

> ❧ letter to Cassandra about Tom Lefroy (but he
> never did, as Jane had hoped, "declare himself")

At length the day is come on which I am to flirt my last with Tom Lefroy, and when you receive this it will be over. My tears flow at the melancholy idea.

> ❧ letter to Cassandra when Jane was twenty-one.
> (Tom's family disapproved of his attraction to the
> penniless neighbor and sent him away to study.)

Where people wish to attach, they should always be ignorant.

> ❧ narrator, who may have learned that the hard way
> *Northanger Abbey*

If a woman doubts as to whether she should accept a man or not, she certainly ought to refuse him. If she can hesitate as to Yes, she ought to say No, directly.

> ❧ Emma, subtly manipulating her young friend
> Harriet *Emma*

A lady's imagination is very rapid; it jumps from admiration to love, from love to matrimony, in a moment.

> ❧ Mr. Darcy *Pride and Prejudice*

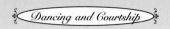

The post-office has a great charm at one period of our lives.

              ◄ Mr. John Knightly, teasing Jane Fairfax *Emma*

If a woman is partial to a man, and does not endeavor to conceal it, he must find it out.

              ◄ Elizabeth, overly optimistic

              Pride and Prejudice

There is meanness in all the arts which ladies sometimes condescend to employ for captivation.

              ◄ Mr. Darcy *Pride and Prejudice*

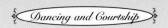

There are very few of us who have heart enough to be really in love without encouragement.

> ❧ Charlotte, resolving to encourage the unappealing
> Mr. Collins *Pride and Prejudice*

Women fancy admiration means more than it does . . . And men take care that they should.

> ❧ Jane and Elizabeth Bennet
> *Pride and Prejudice*

The enthusiasm of a woman's love is even beyond the biographer's.

> ❧ narrator *Mansfield Park*

Next to being married, a girl likes to be crossed in love a little now and then.

       ❧ the sardonic Mr. Bennet, who was mistaken
       Pride and Prejudice

You are too sensible a girl, Lizzy, to fall in love merely because you are warned against it.

       ❧ sensible Aunt Gardiner *Pride and Prejudice*

No man is offended by another man's admiration of the woman he loves.

       ❧ Henry Tilney *Northanger Abbey*

It really was too much to hope even of Harriet, that she could be in love with more than three men in one year.

❧ Emma, worrying about Harriet's future *Emma*

He is so very much occupied by the idea of not being in love with her, that I should not wonder if it were to end in his being so at last.

❧ Mrs. Weston *Emma*

Marianne would have felt herself very inexcusable had she been able to sleep at all the first night after parting from Willoughby.

❧ narrator *Sense and Sensibility*

All the privilege I claim for my own sex (it is not a very enviable one, you need not covet) is that of loving longest, when existence or when hope is gone.

&s Anne Elliot *Persuasion*

Harriet was one of those who, having once begun, would be always in love.

&s Emma, meditating on her young friend *Emma*

I have never yet found that the advice of a sister could prevent a young man's being in love if he chose it.

&s wicked Susan Vernon *Lady Susan*

MARRIAGE

Jane Austen never married, and if she had, she'd never have been free to write the novels we treasure. Three of her sisters-in-law, for that matter, died in childbirth. Nevertheless, she rewarded her heroines, as they learned the lessons they needed, with happy endings in marriage.

When any two young people take it into their heads to marry, they are pretty sure . . . to carry their point, be they ever so poor . . . or ever so little likely to be necessary to each other's ultimate comfort.

❧ narrator *Persuasion*

Miss Bigg . . . writes me word that Miss Blachford is married, but I have never seen it in the Paper. And one may be as well be single, if the Wedding is not to be in print.

                           ✽ letter to Cassandra

It is always incomprehensible to a man, that a woman should ever refuse an offer of marriage. A man always imagines a woman to be ready for anybody who asks her.

              ✽ Emma, defensive about having manipulated her

              young friend to refuse a young farmer *Emma*

Marriage

Anything is to be preferred or endured rather than marrying without affection.

> ❧ letter to niece Fanny, after Jane herself broke her
> engagement to a wealthy neighbor because she could
> not love him

A woman is not to marry a man merely because she is asked, or because he is attached to her.

> ❧ Emma Woodhouse *Emma*

You like him well enough to marry, but not well enough to wait.

> ❧ letter to young Fanny Knight, who had asked for
> advice

Marriage

It is better to know as little as possible of the defects of the person with whom you are to pass your life.

      🐦 Charlotte, seriously unmarried at twenty-seven,

      who later accepted the odious Mr. Collins

      Pride and Prejudice

Dr. Gardiner was married yesterday to Mrs. Percy and her three daughters.

      🐦 letter to Cassandra

His temper might perhaps be a little soured by finding . . . that through some unaccountable bias in favor of beauty, he was the husband of a very silly woman.

      🐦 narrator *Persuasion*

There is not one in a hundred of either sex, who is not taken in when they marry.

        sophisticated and cynical Mary Crawford

Mansfield Park

How wretched, and how unpardonable, how hopeless and how wicked it was, to marry without affection.

        young and high-minded Fanny Price

Mansfield Park

Husbands and wives generally understand when opposition will be vain.

        narrator Persuasion

Matrimony, as the origin of change, was always disagreeable.

> ❧ opinion of Mr. Woodhouse, who was so timid he
>> feared even a new shape for his dining room table
>>> *Emma*

I would rather be Teacher at a school (and I can think
of nothing worse) than marry a man I did not like.

> ❧ Emma Watson *The Watsons* (unfinished novel)

People that marry can never part, but must go and keep house together.

> ❧ naive young Catherine Morland, explaining the
> difference between dancing and matrimony
> *Northanger Abbey*

What is the difference, in matrimonial affairs, between the mercenary and the prudent motive?

> ❧ Elizabeth Bennet, asking the question that
> runs through all Jane Austen's novels
> *Pride and Prejudice*

MONEY

In Jane Austen's world, the question of marriage was linked to that of money. She accepted the fact that while it was wrong to marry for money, it was foolish to marry without it, and took pains to provide at least "a competence" for each couple at the end of a novel. In her novels people received an allowance from parents, inherited money, or married it. Only in her final completed novel, *Persuasion*, did someone—Captain Wentworth—resolve to go out and seek his fortune; times were changing.

Money

There are certainly not so many men of large fortune in the world, as there are pretty women to deserve them.

               ❧ narrator *Northanger Abbey*

I find, on looking into my affairs, that instead of being very rich I am likely to be very poor . . . It is as well . . . to prepare you for the sight of a sister sunk in poverty, that it may not overcome your spirits.

                    ❧ letter to Cassandra

Single women have a dreadful propensity for being poor.

        ❧ advice to her niece Fanny Knight, from a woman
                        who was single and poor

People always live for ever when there is any annuity to be paid them.

    🍂 rich and stingy Fanny Dashwood

    Sense and Sensibility

Every neighborhood should have a great Lady.

    🍂 narrator *Sanditon* (the cheerful unfinished novel

    Jane Austen was working on during her last illness)

What have wealth or grandeur to do with happiness? . . . Grandeur has but little . . . but wealth has much to do with it.

    🍂 sensible Elinor Dashwood

    Sense and Sensibility

They will not come often, I dare say. They live in a handsome style and are rich, and she seemed to like to be rich, and we gave her to understand that we were far from being so; she will soon feel therefore that we are not worth her acquaintance.

           🥬 letter to Cassandra

Those who have not more, must be satisfied with what they have.

           🥬 wealthy self-satisfied Mrs. Rushworth
           Mansfield Park

A narrow income has a tendency to contract the mind, and sour the temper.

🔊 Emma Woodhouse, who had plenty of money

Emma

He is extremely disagreeable and I hate him more than any body else in the world . . . He has a large fortune . . . but then he is very healthy. In short I do not know what to do.

🔊 Miss Stanhope *The Three Sisters* (from the high-spirited juvenilia Jane Austen wrote in her teens)

RIGHT AND WRONG

Jane Austen seldom referred to organized religion, but her family took pains to describe her as a pious Christian. Her father and many of her uncles, cousins, and brothers were clergymen, and she herself wrote three prayers for home services. She had a strong sense of right and wrong, which never wavers in her novels. A famous British statesman once announced that his guiding principle when he wasn't sure what to do was, "What would Jane Austen have said?"

There is one thing, Emma, which a man can always do, if he chuses, and that is, his duty.

᪣ Mr. Knightly *Emma*

It is very unfair to judge of anybody's conduct without an intimate knowledge of their situation.

᪣ Emma, defending her friend Frank *Emma*

Those who tell their own story must be listened to with caution.

᪣ Mr. Parker *Sanditon*

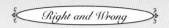

General benevolence, but not general friendship, made a man what he ought to be.

          ❧ Emma Woodhouse, a bit of a snob *Emma*

Pride relates more to our opinion of ourselves, vanity to what we would have others think of us.

          ❧ Mary *Pride and Prejudice*

I do not want people to be very agreeable, as it saves me the trouble of liking them a great deal.

          ❧ letter to Cassandra

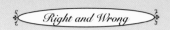
Right and Wrong

Nothing is more deceitful than the appearance of humility. It is often only carelessness of opinion, and sometimes an indirect boast.

❧ Mr. Darcy *Pride and Prejudice*

Here I am once more in this scene of dissipation and vice [London], and I begin already to find my morals corrupted.

❧ letter to Cassandra

Nobody minds having what is too good for them.

❧ narrator *Mansfield Park*

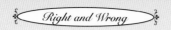

Right and Wrong

Seldom, very seldom, does complete truth belong to any human disclosure; seldom can it happen that something is not disguised, or a little mistaken.

                 narrator *Emma*

I must say that I have seen nobody on the stage who has been a more interesting character than that compound of cruelty and lust.

                 letter to Cassandra after seeing the play

                         "Don Juan"

For what do we live, but to make sport for our neighbours, and laugh at them in our turn?

                 the sardonic Mr. Bennet *Pride and Prejudice*

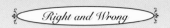

I always deserve the best treatment, because I never put up with any other.

❧ self-confident Emma Woodhouse *Emma*

Elinor agreed to it all, for she did not think he deserved the compliment of rational opposition.

❧ narrator *Sense and Sensibility*

Do not let us be frightened from a good deed by a trifle.

❧ Mrs. Norris, who volunteered others to do the good deeds. *Mansfield Park*

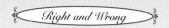

One man's ways may be as good as another's, but we all like our own best.

        &s admirable Admiral Crawford *Persuasion*

As I do not choose to have generosity dictated to me, I shall not resolve on giving my cabinet to Anna till the first thought of it has been my own.

        &s letter to Cassandra

If we feel for the wretched, enough to do all we can for them, the rest is empty sympathy, only distressing to ourselves.

        &s Emma Woodhouse, young, rich, and handsome

                                           Emma

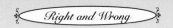

Wisdom is better than Wit, and in the long run will certainly have the laugh on her side.

> ❧ letter to niece Fanny Knight

There are people, who the more you do for them, the less they will do for themselves.

> ❧ Emma, busy trying to make matches for obstinate nonlovers *Emma*

Nobody, who has not been in the interior of a family, can say what the difficulties of any individual of that family may be.

> ❧ Emma *Emma*

HEALTH

In a day when nursing was a large part of a woman's role in life, Jane Austen's letters show a keen interest in medical matters. "How does the corpse appear?" she asks. Announcing their father's death to her brother, she goes into great detail about his last hours. In the novels, when someone is ill, the apothecary is called, or for someone wealthier or sicker, a surgeon. Women of the family, nevertheless, provided most of the health care.

People do not die of trifling little colds.

✎ Mrs. Bennet *Pride and Prejudice*

My sore throats, you know, are always worse than anybody's.

> ❧ whiny Mary Musgrove *Persuasion*

What dreadful hot weather we have! — It keeps one in
a continual state of inelegance.

> ❧ letter to Cassandra (although Jane Austen died
> before Victoria came to the throne, this delicate way
> of indicating she was sweating does make her
> sound — for once — Victorian)

Where health is at stake nothing else should be considered.

> ✒ Mr. Woodhouse, who seldom considered anything else at all *Emma*

A large dish of rather weak cocoa, every evening, agrees with me better than any thing.

> ✒ Arthur Parker, the young hypochondriac about whom Jane Austen made jokes in her unfinished last novel, even as she herself was dying *Sanditon*

FOOD

Jane Austen's family had few servants, and she was intimately involved in planning meals, if not in making them. At one point she was in charge of the family's breakfasts, and of doling out the expensive, locked-away supplies of tea and sugar.

An egg boiled very soft is not unwholesome.

        Mr. Woodhouse, who was afraid of almost every good thing to eat Emma

Good apple pies are a considerable part of our domestic happiness.

⋯ letter to Cassandra

Miss Bates, let Emma help you to a *little* bit of tart — a very little bit . . . I do not advise the custard.

⋯ nervous Mr. Woodhouse *Emma*

I think it [toast] a very bad thing for the stomach. Without a little butter to soften it, it hurts the coats of the stomach.

⋯ greedy Arthur Parker, always playing the invalid

Sanditon

Food

You know how interesting the purchase of a sponge-cake is to me.

🕊 letter to Cassandra

I always take care to provide such things as please my own appetite . . . I have had some ragout veal, and I mean to have some haricot mutton tomorrow.

🕊 letter to Cassandra

LETTERS TO CASSANDRA

In an age when letter writing was an art and a respected way of filling up one's time, Jane Austen excelled in the practice. Fortunately for us, she and her sister were often separated when one made long visits to brothers or friends (while the other, of course, had to stay home as companion to their parents). After the author's death, Cassandra burned any letters that contained sharp comments about family members, but enough remains for us to delight in a witty picture of everyday life in the late eighteenth and early nineteenth century.

Letters to Cassandra

What a pleasure it must have been to receive letters from Jane Austen!

I will not say that your mulberry-trees are dead, but I am afraid they are not alive.

❦

At the bottom of Kingsdown Hill we met a gentleman in a buggy, who, on minute examination, turned out to be Dr. Hall —and Dr. Hall in such very deep mourning that either his mother, his wife, or himself must be dead.

I shall not tell you anything more of Wm. Digweed's china, as your silence on the subject makes you unworthy of it.

Mrs. B. and two young women were of the same party, except when Mrs. B. thought herself obliged to leave them to run round the room after her drunken husband. His avoidance, and her pursuit, with the probable intoxication of both, was an amusing scene.

❧❧❧

You express so little anxiety about my being murdered under Ash Park Copse by Mrs. Hulbert's servant, that I have a great mind not to tell you whether I was or not.

❧❦❧

I am proud to say that I have a very good eye at any adultress, for tho' repeatedly assured that another in the same party was the *She*, I fixed upon the right one from the first.

I do not like the Miss Blackstones; indeed, I was always determined not to like them, so there is the less merit in it.

❧❦❧

You deserve a longer letter than this; but it is my unhappy fate seldom to treat people so well as they deserve.

Expect a most agreeable letter, for not being overbur-
dened with subject (having nothing at all to say), I shall
have no check to my genius from beginning to end.

We have been exceedingly busy ever since you went away. In the first place we have had to rejoice two or three times every day at your having such very delightful weather for the whole of your journey . . .

❧⚜❧

Your silence on the subject of our ball makes me suppose your curiosity too great for words.

We plan on having a steady cook and a young, giddy housemaid, with a sedate, middle-aged man, who is to undertake the double office of husband to the former and sweetheart to the latter. No children, of course, to be allowed on either side.

On Her Writing

Women who belonged to the gentry, as Jane Austen did, were not expected to earn money, and certainly not by writing novels. Her first works were published "by a Lady" and then "by the Author of Sense and Sensibility." The lengthy inscription her loving family chose for her tombstone makes no mention of her writing.

In an age when novels featured kidnappings, duels, and the new governess who arrives at the dark castle door in a thunderstorm, she wrote about daily life as she knew it, with no dukes, no dungeons, and no sadistic villains. Her characters are so real that two hundred years later, Internet discussion

groups argue endlessly about whether Charlotte should have married Mr. Collins and why it is that no one really likes Fanny Price.

More than one critic has placed her second only to Shakespeare.

I must confess that I think her [heroine Elizabeth Bennet in *Pride and Prejudice*] as delightful a character as ever appeared in print.

                  ❧ letter to Cassandra

3 or 4 Families in a country village is the very thing to work on.

           ❧ advice to niece Anna, who was writing a novel

You may perhaps like her [heroine Fanny Price in *Mansfield Park*]; she is almost too good for me.

         ❧ letter to Cassandra

I think I may boast myself to be, with all possible vanity, the most unlearned and uninformed female who ever dared to be an authoress.

         ❧ letter (tongue in cheek?) to a ridiculous clergyman
         who wanted her to write the history of a German
         royal house

I think she will like my [heroine] Elinor, but cannot build on anything else.

         ❧ letter to Cassandra

I am going to take a heroine [Emma] whom no one but myself will much like.

🌱 as told to her family

My own darling child [her novel *Pride and Prejudice*] is come from London.

🌱 letter to Cassandra

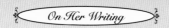

. . . the little bit (two inches wide) of ivory on which I work with so fine a brush, as produces little effect after much labour.

> ❧ letter to nephew Edward, who was also writing a novel (many years later he became her first biographer)

I am never too busy to think of [her novel *Sense and Sensibility*]. I can no more forget it, than a mother can forget her sucking child.

> ❧ letter to Cassandra

GROWING OLD

n Jane Austen's day women grew old earlier than they do now. It's clear from her novels that women in their twenties were already a bit shopworn in the marriage market. Her nephew tells us that Jane and her sister Cassandra started wearing the indoor caps that marked middle-aged and old ladies, in their early thirties.

I bought a Concert Ticket and a sprig of flowers for my old age.

❧ letter to Cassandra when Jane was thirty-eight
and had only three more years to live

Growing Old

It was the same room in which we danced fifteen years ago! I thought it all over, and in spite of the shame of being so much older, felt with thankfulness that I was quite as happy now as then.

❧ letter to Cassandra when Jane was thirty-three

Mrs. Bates . . . was a very old lady, almost past everything but tea and quadrille [a card game, not the dance].

❧ narrator Emma

Anne hoped she had outgrown the age of blushing, but the age of emotion she had not.

❧ narrator Persuasion

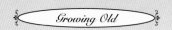

[I] am very well satisfied with his notice of me—"A pleasing-looking young woman"—that must do; one cannot pretend to anything better now; thankful to have it continued a few years longer!

> ❧ letter to Cassandra when Jane was thirty-six

It sometimes happens that a woman is handsomer at twenty-nine than she was ten years before. If there has been neither ill-health nor anxiety, it is a time of life at which scarcely any charm is lost.

> ❧ narrator, about the stately Elizabeth
>
> *Persuasion*

By the bye, as I must leave off being young, I find many Douceurs in being a sort of chaperon [at dances], for I am put on the Sofa near the Fire & can drink as much wine as I like.

      ❧ letter to Cassandra when Jane was thirty-seven

. . . my dearest sister, my tender, watchful, indefatigable nurse, has not been made ill by her exertions. As to what I owe to her, and to the anxious affection of all my beloved family on this occasion, I can only cry over it and pray to God to bless them more and more.

      ❧ letter to Frances Tilson, two months before Jane
         Austen's death at the age of forty-one

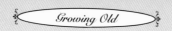

I must not depend upon being ever very blooming again. Sickness is a dangerous indulgence at my time of life.

         ➳ *letter to niece Fanny, three months before the*
         author's death

If I live to be an old woman I must expect to wish I had died now, blessed in the tenderness of such a family, and before I had survived either them or their affection.

         ➳ *letter to her friend Anne Sharp, two months*
         before her death